MY FIRST
PAINT
B·O·O·K

DAWN SIRETT

Stoddart

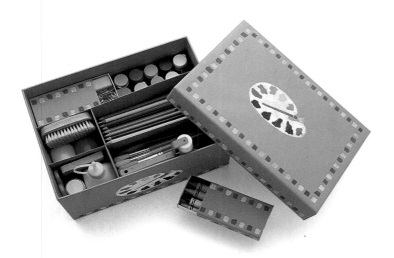

DK
A Dorling Kindersley Book

Designer *Mandy Earey*
Photography *Dave King*
Production *Ruth Cobb*

Managing Editor *Jane Yorke*
Managing Art Editor *Chris Scollen*

First published in Canada in 1994 by
Stoddart Publishing Co. Limited
34 Lesmill Road, Toronto, Canada, M3B 2T6

First published in Great Britain in 1994
by Dorling Kindersley Limited,
9 Henrietta Street, London WC2E 8PS

Canadian Cataloguing in Publication Data

Sirett, Dawn
My first paint book

ISBN 0-7737-2777-9

1. Painting – Technique – Juvenile literature.
2. Handicraft – Juvenile literature. I. Title.

TT160.S57 1994   j745.7   C93-095080-1

Dorling Kindersley would like to thank the following for
their help in producing this book: Jane Bull for making the
projects on pages 26, 36, and 39, Mark Richards for jacket design,
Jonathan Buckley, and Rosemary Sirett. Dorling Kindersley
would also like to give special thanks to the following for
appearing in this book: Victoria Chandler, Josey Edwards,
Jade McNamara, Keat Ng, and Tebedge Ricketts.

Illustrations by Brian Delf

Color reproduction by Colourscan, Singapore
Printed and bound in Italy by L.E.G.O.

CONTENTS

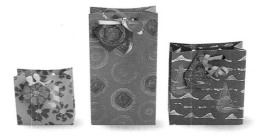

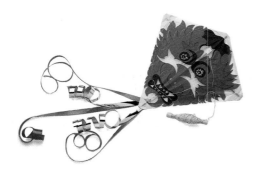

PAINTING BY PICTURES

My First Paint Book shows you how to make and paint all sorts of wonderful things using everyday materials. Step-by-step photographs and simple instructions tell you exactly what to do, and there are life-size photographs of all the finished projects. On the opposite page is a list of things to remember when using this book, and below are the points to look for on each page when making and painting the projects.

How to use this book

What the project is about
The introduction to each project tells you important information about the activity shown.

Equipment
Illustrated checklists show you which tools you will need to have ready before you start each project.

The materials you need
The items to collect for each project are shown life-size to help you check that you have everything you will need.

PERFECT PRINTS

Printing is a fun way to use paint and the results look great. Thick, sticky paint works best. All sorts of things such as card, vegetables, or even your fingers can be used as printing tools. A sponge on an old cookie sheet makes a good printing pad. To avoid mixing colors, use one tool for each color and let the first color dry when printing one color over another. Try decorating writing paper and envelopes. You can also print on invitations, greeting cards, or postcards.

EQUIPMENT

Sharp knife

Scissors

Cookie sheet

Household sponges

Jar of water

You will need

Writing paper

Poster paints

Paintbrush

Printing tools

Small matchbox

Large and small carrots

Button

Cotton swab

Envelopes

A piece of thin household sponge

Plastic drinking straw

Large and small cardboard tubes

Thick cardboard

Corrugated cardboard

Printing the paper

1 Put some damp sponges on an old cookie sheet. Pour paint and some water onto the sponges.* Spread out the paint with a brush.

2 Ask an adult to cut the carrots. Cut a sponge shape. Press each tool into the paint and press firmly on the paper to make a print.**

3 Print with different colors and tools to make a pattern or picture on the paper. Put more paint on each tool every few prints.

*The paint needs to be thick and sticky.
**Practice on scrap paper first.

The finished prints
Try printing a border, a stamp mark, or a picture on the paper and envelopes. Make sure you leave space to write in!

Tree prints made with sponge and the edge of cardboard

Ground printed with the edge of corrugated cardboard

Circle print made with a cardboard tube

Pattern printed with a button and a small tube

Border printed with a triangular piece of sponge

Circle prints made with a cotton swab and a straw

Tractor printed with carrots, a matchbox, the edge of cardboard, and a cotton swab

Things to remember

1 Read through all the instructions before you begin a project and gather together everything you will need.

2 Put on an apron or an old shirt before you start and roll up your sleeves.

3 Lay down lots of newspaper to protect worktables and the floor.

4 Be very careful when using scissors or sharp knives. **Do not use them unless an adult is there to help you.**

5 Always open the windows when using oil-based glaze. Ask an adult to clean the brush in mineral spirits for you.

6 Put everything away when you have finished and clean up any mess.

Step by step
Step-by-step photographs and clear instructions tell you exactly what to do at each stage of a project.

Painting tips
Look out for useful tips, which give you extra information about a painting technique.

The finished project
Life-size photographs show you what the finished projects look like, helping you make them.

PAINTED BOTTLES

Try turning empty bottles or jars into pretty vases and pots. Clean and dry the bottles or jars before you paint them. You can paint glass or plastic, but be very careful with glass: keep the bottle or jar on a table while you paint it. Finish with a coat of glaze so the paint doesn't rub off.

EQUIPMENT

Jar of water   Saucer

You will need

Medium paintbrush

Thin paintbrush

Poster paints

Empty bottles or jars (plastic or glass)

Clear glaze

White glue

Painting the bottle

1 Make sure the bottle or jar is clean and dry. Mix some white glue with the paint. This helps the paint stick to the glass or plastic.

2 Paint a design on the bottle or jar. A simple idea is to dab on dots of paint all over the bottle. Try using lots of different colors.

3 When the paint is dry, paint clear glaze on the bottle or jar. This will protect the paint and give a shiny finish.

The finished bottles and jars
The finished jars and bottles make perfect vases, pencil pots, or brush pots, and are excellent gifts for friends and family.

A border around the rim adds the finishing touch.

Here, one color has been painted into another.

PAINTING TIPS
• Keep the paint fairly thick so that it doesn't run.
• If you make a mistake, wipe the paint off before it dries and start again.

You can cover the container completely, or leave some glass or plastic showing.

A simple pattern of zigzags, dots, and circles suits this narrow jar.

18   19

PAINTING KIT

Here you see the tools and equipment that you will need to paint the projects in this book. For most of the activities you can use poster paints, but for some you will need special paints, such as fabric or marbling paints, which you can buy in arts and crafts stores. Some of the projects are painted with sponges or nailbrushes instead of paintbrushes, and in other projects, pictures or patterns are scratched into paint with plastic knives or forks.

Rags are very useful for cleaning your paintbrushes and other equipment. You will need lots of newspaper to keep your work area clean.

Fabric paints

Marbling paints

Newspaper

Poster paints

Acrylic paints usually come in tubes like this.

Clear glaze (or polyurethane) seals and protects paint.*

Acrylic paints

Even if you only have a few paints, you can make more colors by mixing them together.

Old saucers make good painting palettes.

Ready-mixed, water-based paints

Ready-mixed, water-based paints often come in large squeeze bottles like this one.

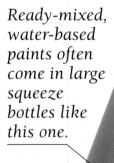

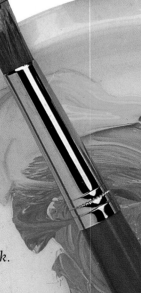
*We have used oil-based glaze for the projects in this book.

Thick paintbrush

Medium paintbrush

Thin paintbrush

Flat paintbrush

Choose thin brushes with pointed ends for painting fine lines.

Rags

Paint large areas with a thick or flat-ended brush.

Stencil brush

Large, flat paintbrush or old pastry brush

Printing roller (You can buy these from arts and crafts stores.)

Thin household sponges can be used for painting and to make printing pads.

Old nailbrush or scrub brush

Plastic knife and fork

Flour for thickening paint

White glue for thickening paint and sticking things

Use an old cookie sheet and a sponge as a printing pad.

Instead of a saucer, you could use an old muffin tin as a palette.

7

PERFECT PRINTS

Printing is a fun way to use paint and the results look great. Thick, sticky paint works best. All sorts of things such as cardboard, vegetables, or even your fingers can be used as printing tools. A sponge on an old cookie sheet makes a good printing pad. To avoid mixing colors, use one tool for each color and let the first color dry when printing one color over another. Try decorating writing paper and envelopes. You can also print on invitations, greeting cards, or postcards.

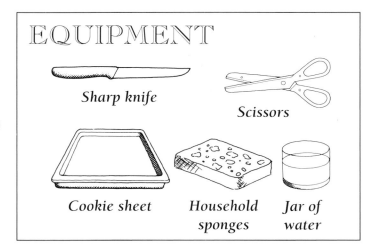

EQUIPMENT

Sharp knife

Scissors

Cookie sheet

Household sponges

Jar of water

You will need

Writing paper

Poster paints

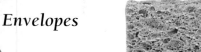

Paintbrush

Printing tools

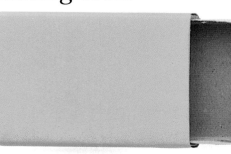

Large and small carrots

Small matchbox

Button

Envelopes

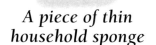

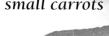

Cotton swab

A piece of thin household sponge

Plastic drinking straw

Large and small cardboard tubes

Thick cardboard

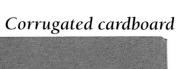

Corrugated cardboard

Printing the paper

1 Put some damp sponges on an old cookie sheet. Pour paint and some water onto the sponges.* Spread out the paint with a brush.

2 Ask an adult to cut the carrots. Cut a sponge shape. Press each tool into the paint and press firmly on the paper to make a print.**

3 Print with different colors and tools to make a pattern or picture on the paper. Put more paint on each tool every few prints.

*The paint needs to be thick and sticky.
**Practice on scrap paper first.

The finished prints

Try printing a border, a stamp mark, or a picture on the paper and envelopes. Make sure you leave space to write in!

Tree prints made with sponge and the edge of cardboard

Ground printed with the edge of corrugated cardboard

Circle print made with a cardboard tube

Pattern printed with a button and a small tube

Border printed with a triangular piece of sponge

Circle prints made with a cotton swab and a straw

Tractor printed with carrots, a matchbox, the edge of cardboard, and a cotton swab

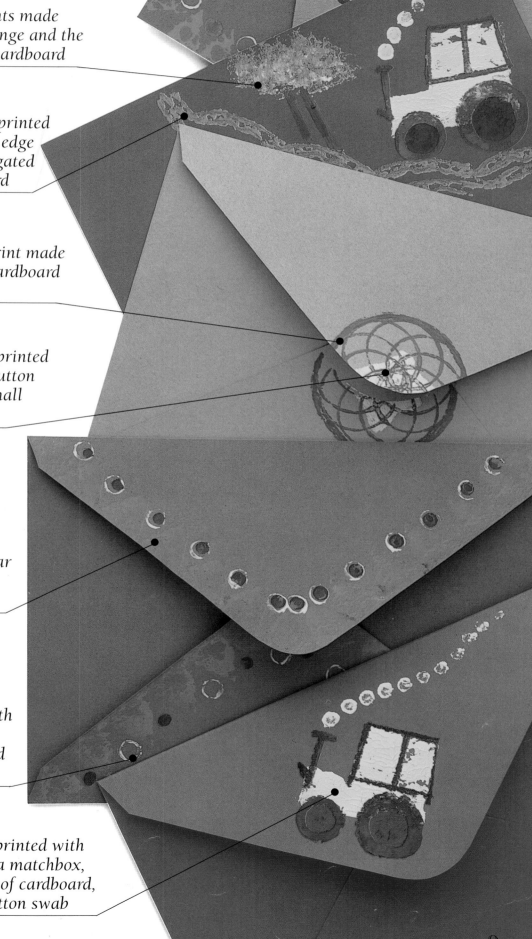

9

GIFT BAGS

Here, you can find out how to make printing blocks from modeling clay and create fabulous patterned paper. Use thick paint, sponges, and an old cookie sheet, as on page 9. You can turn your printed paper into gift bags, or simply use the sheets as wrapping paper. The gift bags are also useful for storing things in.

EQUIPMENT

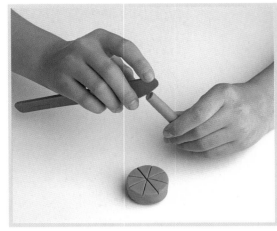

Pencil

Scissors

Hole punch

Cookie sheet and household sponges

Ruler

Jar of water

You will need

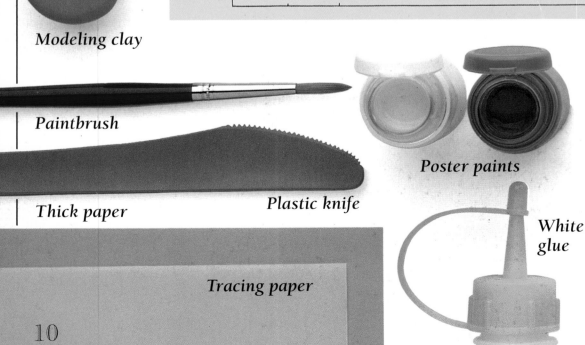

Gift ribbon

Modeling clay

Paintbrush

Thick paper

Plastic knife

Poster paints

Tracing paper

White glue

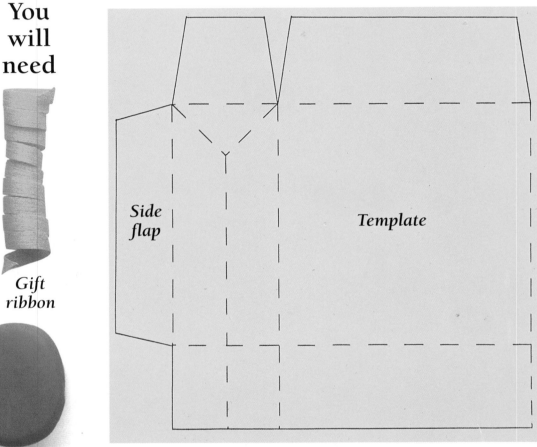

Side flap

Template

10

Making the gift bag

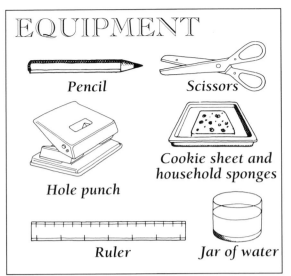

1 Shape a lump of modeling clay. Flatten one side and make marks in it. Use different shaped lumps to make different prints.*

2 Press the clay into the printing pad. Then print a pattern on a sheet of paper. Leave the paint to dry before printing a new color.

3 Trace the template onto tracing paper with a pencil. Then color over the lines with the pencil, as shown.

Here, dots are made in a roll of clay and crossed lines are made in a round lump.

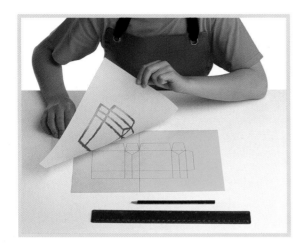

4 Turn the tracing paper over. Place it on the back of the dry printed sheet of paper. Draw over the template twice, as shown.**

5 Cut out the bag pattern. Score along the lines and fold them, as shown, to make the bag. Glue the side flap and let it dry.

6 Glue the bottom flaps. You can put something heavy in the bag to help them stick. When dry, punch two holes in the top.

The finished gift bags

Here are some ideas for patterns and colors to print. Gold paint makes an extra special bag. You can make different sized bags by changing the size of the template.

The printing block for the circles was made by pressing a button into a round lump of clay.

Boats and waves

For this block, the outline of a boat was marked into clay and then the extra clay was cut off.

For the waves block, the outline of waves was marked into clay and then the clay around the outline was cut away.

A diamond was marked into a square of clay to make the printing block for the blue diamonds.

GIFT TAGS

Cut out small rectangles of the paper and fold them to make tags. You can then cut the folded rectangles into other shapes, if you wish. Use a hole punch to make a hole for the ribbon.

Flowers

Circles and diamonds

eave off the side flap the second time you draw over the lines of the template.

11

WONDERFUL WAX

Wax and paint do not mix, but they can be used together to create an exciting picture. Here, thick paint is painted over wax crayon and then scratched off to make a picture of colorful fireworks. You can scratch out a nighttime scene, an animal, a pattern, or anything you like. Find out how to frame your picture on page 46.

how to frame your picture on page 46.

EQUIPMENT

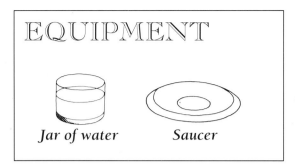

Jar of water   *Saucer*

You will need

Light-colored paper

Black poster paint

Popsicle stick

Plastic knife

Thin paintbrush

Thick paintbrush

Wax crayons

Making the picture

1 Use brightly colored wax crayons to draw a pattern on a sheet of paper. Fill the sheet of paper with the pattern.

2 Paint over the pattern with thick black paint. Make sure the pattern is completely covered. You may need two coats of paint.

3 When the paint is dry, draw a picture by scratching off the paint with a plastic knife, a stick, or the end of a paintbrush.

The finished picture

When the black paint is scratched off, you can see the crayon underneath. Bright colors show up well, so use as many brightly colored crayons as you can to make the pattern.

You can find out how to scratch shapes into wet paint on page 44. The marks on the frame were made in this way.

You can use the popsicle stick to scrape off large areas of paint.

The end of a paintbrush makes a medium mark.

Painted card frame

Zigzags, swirls, and stars make brilliant, exploding fireworks!

FRAME IT!
A frame adds the finishing touch to a picture. You can find out how to make picture frames on page 46.

Thin or thick marks can be scratched out with the plastic knife.

13

STENCIL DESIGNS

Stenciling is a fun way to repeat a picture or pattern. A stencil is a piece of card with shapes cut out of it. To stencil, you hold the card flat on a surface and paint through the holes.

You can stencil on walls, furniture, or fabrics, but check with an adult first. Below, a palette and border of squares are stenciled on an art box. You can make up a picture or pattern to stencil. Always leave some cardboard around your designs and glaze the stencils to make them long-lasting.

Practice using your stencils on scrap paper. You will need thick poster paints or acrylic paints and a stencil brush or a sponge to paint with.

A piece of thin household sponge

EQUIPMENT

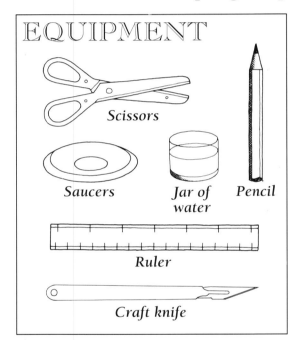

Scissors

Saucers

Jar of water

Pencil

Ruler

Craft knife

You will need

Clear glaze

Paintbrush for glazing the stencils

Stencil brush (or a brush with short, stiff hairs)

Poster paints (or you can use acrylic paints)

Making the box

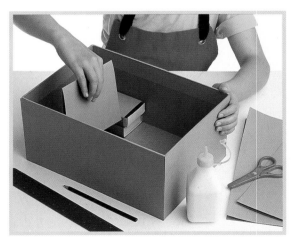

1 Cut two pieces of cardboard to fit the length of the box. Make them twice the depth of the box and fold them in half, as shown.

2 Paint or cover two matchboxes. Cut a length of cardboard to go across the box.* Make it twice the depth and fold it in half, as before.

The cardboard should fit across the box from one side to the matchboxes, as shown.

3 Cut a slit half way down one long partition and another half way up the short partition, so that they slot together, as shown.

14

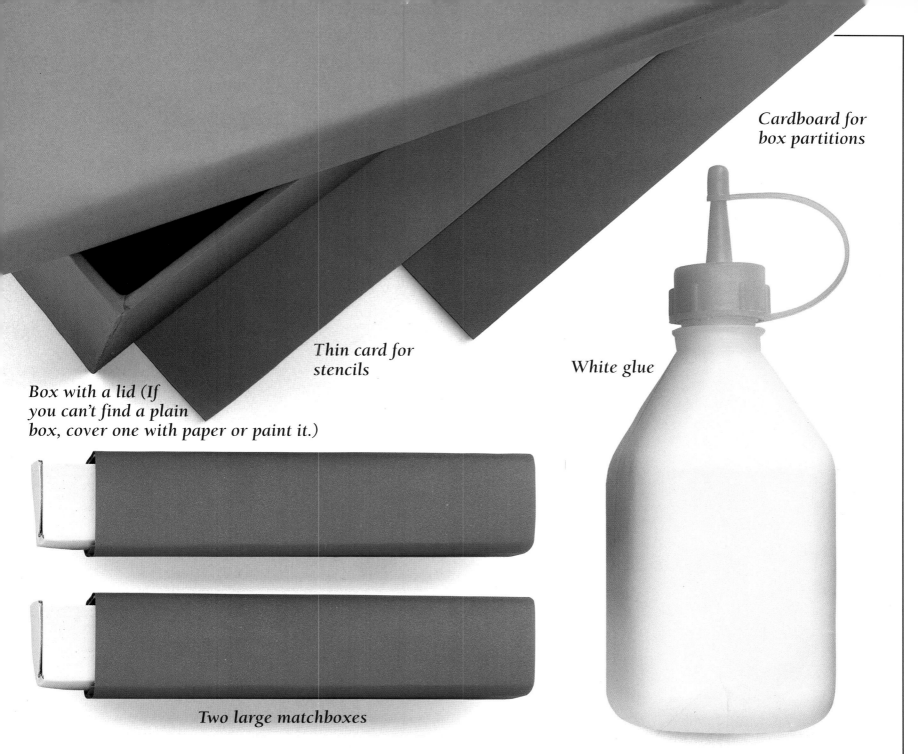

Cardboard for
box partitions

Thin card for
stencils

White glue

Box with a lid (If
you can't find a plain
box, cover one with paper or paint it.)

Two large matchboxes

Stenciling the box

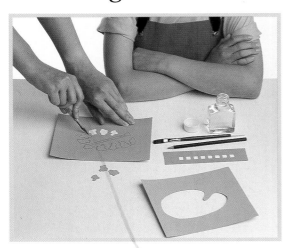

1 Draw a pattern or picture on a
piece of cardboard. Ask an
adult to cut out your design. Glaze
both sides and leave it to dry.

2 Decide where you want your
design to go on the box. Hold
the stencil flat.** Paint in the holes
with a stencil brush or sponge.

**If you find it hard to hold the stencil in
place, tape it down with masking tape.

3 You can use more than one
stencil to make a picture
or pattern. Wait for the first color
to dry before stenciling over it.

15

STENCILED ART BOX

Your stenciled design can be repeated on each side of the art box, on the lid, and on the matchboxes, too. You can fill the box with all kinds of painting and drawing equipment. The bigger compartments can hold paintbrushes, paints, and pencils. The matchboxes are perfect for paper clips, erasers, or crayons. You might have room for other items, such as your scissors and roller, sponges, modeling tools, modeling clay, and glaze. The box could also be used to store jewelry, sewing equipment, or a collection.

Matchboxes make small compartments. Use as many as you need.

The three partitions divide the box into large and small compartments, which can hold different sized objects.

A PLACE FOR EVERYTHING

Before you cut out your partitions, put everything you want the art box to hold into the box. This will help you decide on the best way to divide up your box.

STENCILING TIPS
• You may find it easier to paint the outside edge of the stencil hole first and work inward.
• To avoid smudging the paint, don't take the stencil away until the paint is dry.
• Use thick, sticky paint so that it doesn't bleed under the stencil.

The line of small red and yellow squares makes a decorative border.

16

Simple shapes work well when
stenciled, such as these squares.

Colorful artist's
palette design

PAINTING THEME
Two stencils were used for the palette design.
First, the palette was stenciled in white
and left to dry. Then the second stencil
was held over the palette and the
blobs of paint and brush were
stenciled on top.

White palette
stenciled first

Paints and
brush stenciled
over palette

Border
of squares

PAINTED BOTTLES

Try turning empty bottles or jars into pretty vases and pots. Clean and dry the bottles or jars before you paint them. You can paint glass or plastic, but be very careful with glass: keep the bottle or jar on a table while you paint it. Finish with a coat of glaze so the paint doesn't rub off.

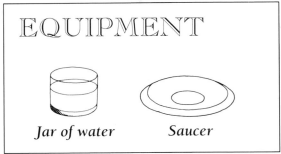
You will need

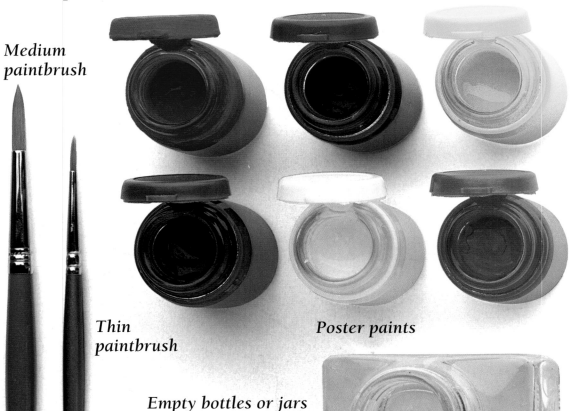

Medium paintbrush

Thin paintbrush

Poster paints

Empty bottles or jars (plastic or glass)

Clear glaze

White glue

Painting the bottle

1 Make sure the bottle or jar is clean and dry. Mix some white glue with the paint. This helps the paint stick to the glass or plastic.

2 Paint a design on the bottle or jar. A simple idea is to dab on dots of paint all over the bottle. Try using lots of different colors.

3 When the paint is dry, paint clear glaze on the bottle or jar. This will protect the paint and give a shiny finish.

18

The finished bottles and jars

The finished jars and bottles make perfect vases, pencil pots, or brush pots, and are excellent gifts for friends and family.

A border around the rim adds the finishing touch.

Here, one color has been painted into another.

PAINTING TIPS

- Keep the paint fairly thick so that it doesn't run.
- If you make a mistake, wipe the paint off before it dries and start again.

You can cover the container completely, or leave some glass or plastic showing.

A simple pattern of zigzags, dots, and circles suits this narrow jar.

19

T-SHIRT PAINTING

Paint your own T-shirts and then wear your original designs! You will be amazed at how easy it is to make them. You can create a unique pattern every time by splattering one color or more onto the fabric. Always remember to lay down lots of newspaper when flicking paint in this way.

You will need special fabric paints for this project. These can be bought from arts and crafts stores. Check the instructions that come with your paints. You may need to ask an adult to iron your T-shirt on the reverse side to fix the paint when it has dried. Turn the page to see the finished splattered T-shirt. You will also find some other ideas for painting on fabric.

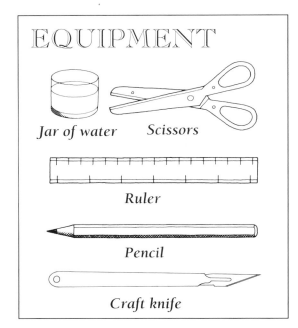

EQUIPMENT

Jar of water   Scissors

Ruler

Pencil

Craft knife

You will need

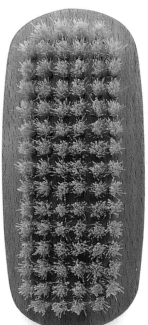

Masking tape

Fabric paints (Choose colors that will show up well on your T-shirt.)

Old nailbrush or scrub brush

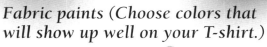

T-shirt

Splattering the T-shirt

Plastic knife

Large, flat brush for flicking paint

Two sheets of corrugated cardboard (slightly larger than the T-shirt)

Paintbrush

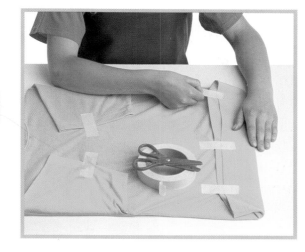

1 Put one sheet of cardboard into the shirt to stop the paint from soaking through.* Tape the sleeves and bottom of the shirt, as shown.

2 Draw a square with 8 in. (20 cm) sides in the middle of another sheet of cardboard. Ask an adult to cut out the square, leaving a frame.

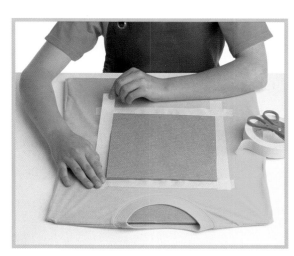

3 Place the cutout square in the middle of the front of the shirt. Mark the position of the square with tape. Then remove the square.

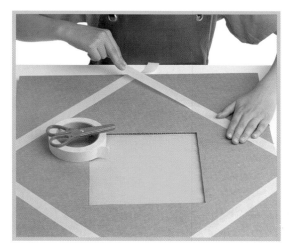

4 Line up the frame with the tape on the T-shirt and tape it down, as shown. Cover any parts of the T-shirt that still show.

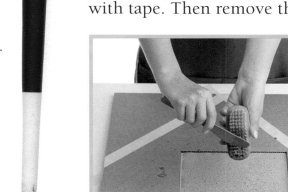

5 Put fabric paint on a nailbrush. Use a plastic knife to flick the paint away from your body, onto the shirt. Leave the paint to dry.

6 Dip a large brush into a new color. Splatter the paint onto the T-shirt. When dry, ask an adult to iron the shirt to fix the paint.**

*Cut the cardboard to fit inside the T-shirt.

**First check the instructions that come with your paints.

21

DAZZLING DESIGNS

Here are three finished T-shirts plus some ideas for other things that you can decorate with fabric paints. Try painting a pair of socks or a baseball cap to match your T-shirt, or use your paints to brighten up old handkerchiefs, pillowcases, tablecloths, or cotton scarves.

As well as splattering on fabric, you can print, stencil, or simply paint a picture with a brush. Turn to pages 8, 10, 14, and 28 for instructions on printing and stenciling.

Printed daisy

SOCKS TO MATCH
Try painting a pair of socks to match your T-shirt.

FABRIC PAINTING TIPS

• Ask an adult to iron the fabric first so that it is completely flat when you paint it.
• Always put a sheet of cardboard under the fabric because the paint will soak through.
• The fabric will absorb a lot of paint so you may need two coats. Leave the first coat to dry before you paint the second.

SPLATTER PATTERN

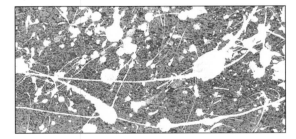

PRINTED DAISIES

STENCILED CAR

Above are the T-shirt designs close-up.

SPLATTERED SQUARE

A little fabric paint goes a long way when splattering. Load your brush with paint and keep splattering and flicking until no more paint comes off.

You can also make a splatter picture on paper. Turn to page 47 to see a framed splatter picture.

When you take away the frame and masking tape, you will be left with a neat splattered square. You can use triangular or round frames to make different shaped designs.

You can splatter the back of the shirt as well as the front.

Printed
polka dots

Stenciled
car

DOTTED HANDKERCHIEF
*Turn a plain cotton handkerchief
into a dotted one. A cotton swab
was used to print this pattern.*

CAP
*Try stenciling
a design on the
bill of a cap.*

VEHICLE
STENCILS
*Three stencils
have been used
on this shirt. The
white rectangles
were sponged on
first. Then the blue
car and truck were
stenciled on top.
Turn to page 14
for instructions
on stenciling.*

DAISY PRINTS
*Modeling clay was
used to make the printing
blocks for the daisies on
this shirt (see page 10
for this technique).
Chains of daisies have
been printed across the
front and back of the
T-shirt and around
the sleeves.*

*You can touch up
any faint prints
with a paintbrush.*

23

PAINTED PEBBLES

Turn pebbles into colorful painted fish and create an amazing underwater world for them to swim in! The pebbles hang in a shallow box on clear fishing line. Look on the beach or in a park for different-sized pebbles or stones and fishlike shapes. Find some pictures of tropical fish to give you ideas on how to paint them. Turn the page to see a finished seascape.

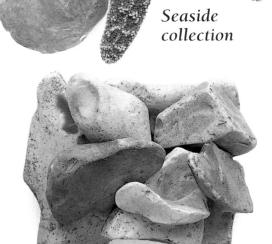
Seaside collection

EQUIPMENT

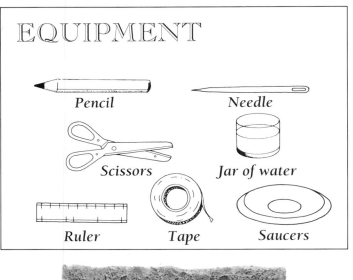

Pencil

Needle

Scissors

Jar of water

Ruler

Tape

Saucers

You will need

Clear glaze

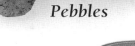
Pebbles

A piece of thin household sponge

Poster paints

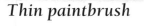
Medium paintbrush

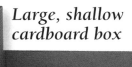
Thin paintbrush

Large, shallow cardboard box

Thin cardboard

Paper

Clear fishing line or thread

White glue

Making the seascape

1 Paint or glue paper over any writing on your box to give it a neat finish. You may need two coats of paint if you paint the box.

2 Paint a sandy seabed and an underwater background on the inside of the box. Try dabbing on paint with a sponge.

3 Draw sea plants and coral on cardboard and cut them out. Fold the bottom of the plants and coral over so they stand up.

4 Paint the plants and coral with a sponge. When dry, glue along the flaps and stick them to the bottom of the box to make a scene.

5 Wash and dry the pebbles. Mix some white paint with glue and use this to paint an undercoat on the pebbles. Leave them to dry.

6 Put the pebbles on a saucer so you can turn them without touching them. Use paints mixed with glue to paint the pebbles.

7 When the paint is dry, glaze the pebbles to protect the paint. When they are dry, tie a length of fishing line around each pebble.*

8 Ask an adult to use a needle to pull the fishing line through the top of the box, as shown.** Tape the ends down.

9 Arrange shells, driftwood, or stones in the base of the box. You can paint sea animals on more pebbles and add these as well.

*We have used black thread to show you what to do. You should use clear fishing line or thread.
**Hold the fish in place first to decide where you want them to hang.

FISHY SCENE

You can keep the finished underwater scene on a table, bookshelf, or windowsill. Use as many fish and shells as you like. If you tap the box gently, all the fish will move, just as if they are swimming in the water!

SETTING THE SCENE

Wait for everything to dry before you assemble the scene. Hang the fish at different levels so that they fill the box.

PLANTS AND CORAL

You can add depth to the scene by positioning large sea plants and coral at the back and smaller ones in the middle and at the front of the box. The fish can swim in between the plants and coral.

SCHOOLS OF FISH

Fish often swim together in groups or "schools." Here the orange, yellow, and blue fish have been arranged into groups.

As well as fish, you can paint sea plants, crabs, or other sea creatures on stones.

Make a seaside collection of shells, stones, small rocks, or driftwood for the seabed.

You can leave some of the box showing to add texture to the scene.

The outside of the box has been covered with blue paper.

If the fishing line slips off the pebbles, use clear tape to hold it in place.

MIXING COLORS

Different shades of blue have been made for the background by mixing different amounts of white with blue paint. The paint has been dabbed on with a sponge.

FABULOUS FISH!

The pebbles were painted in two stages. The base color was painted first. Once dry, eyes, fins, and scales were painted on top with a thin brush.

The plants and coral were painted by dabbing on orange, green, and white paint with a sponge. Try sponging one color over another.

27

ANIMAL FRIEZE

Here, you can find out how to make printing blocks by gluing string onto cardboard. You can use the blocks to print a frieze to go around the walls of your room. Try making a printing block of your favorite animal. Keep the string picture simple – just an outline is best.

EQUIPMENT

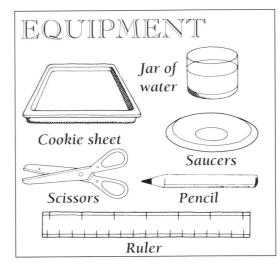

Jar of water

Cookie sheet

Saucers

Scissors

Pencil

Ruler

You will need

Thick colored paper

Thick cardboard

Thin string

A piece of thin household sponge

White glue

Cotton swab

Paintbrush

Leaves

Printing roller

Ready-mixed, water-based paints*

You can buy these in large squeeze bottles (see page 6).

Making the blocks

1 Draw the outline of an animal on a piece of cardboard. You can draw any animal, or trace the elephants on the next page.

2 Glue lengths of string to the outline. Use shorter lengths for eyes and ears. When the glue is dry, cut around the animal.

3 To finish the printing block, glue the string animal to another piece of cardboard, as shown. Leave it to dry.

Printing the frieze

1 Put some paint on an old cookie sheet. Paint the string printing block with a printing roller or a wide paintbrush.

2 Place the block facedown on a long strip of thick paper. Press down firmly on the back of the block. Then lift it up carefully.

3 Print enough animals to fill the paper. You can use leaves, a sponge, some cardboard, and a cotton swab to print a background.

The finished frieze

In this frieze, the trunks and tails of the elephants link to make a chain!

Red and green paints were mixed together to make brown.

Try painting the back of leaves with a brush and then printing them on the paper.

You can use a larger or smaller animal to start and finish the frieze.

Tusks painted with a cotton swab

Grass printed with the edge of card

Branches painted with a cotton swab

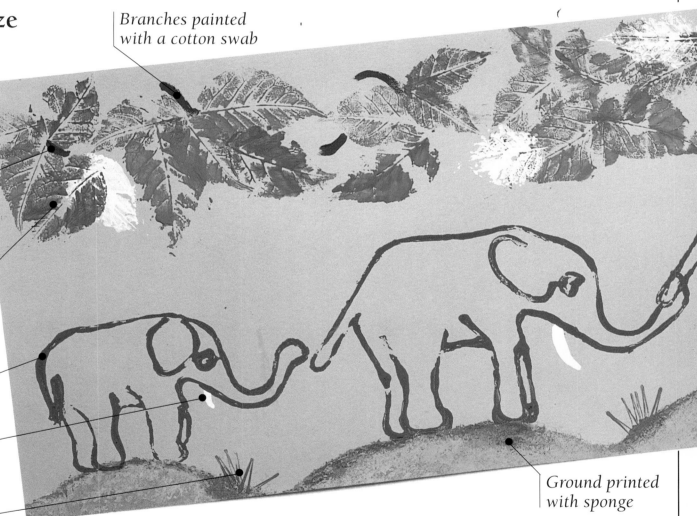

Ground printed with sponge

STRING PRINTING TIPS
• Practice on scrap paper first.
• It may take a couple of coats of paint before your string block will print because the string may absorb a lot of paint.
• If there are gaps in some of your prints, fill them in with a paintbrush.

ELEPHANTS ON THE MARCH
You can make the frieze as long or as short as you want.

A Diamond Kite

Make, paint, and fly a colorful kite with a wonderful dragon-face design! The kite is made from a large plastic bag. Look for a bag without any writing on it, such as a large garbage bag. Acrylic paints work best on plastic. If you don't have these, you can mix some white glue with poster paint, but you may find that some of the paint peels off the plastic.

Plant stakes are used for the kite spars. They make a frame for the plastic. Medium-sized stakes, 18 in. (46 cm) long, should be the correct size. If they are too long, ask an adult to trim them.

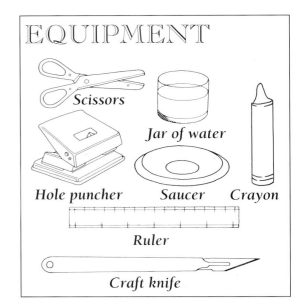

EQUIPMENT

Scissors

Jar of water

Hole puncher

Saucer

Crayon

Ruler

Craft knife

You will need

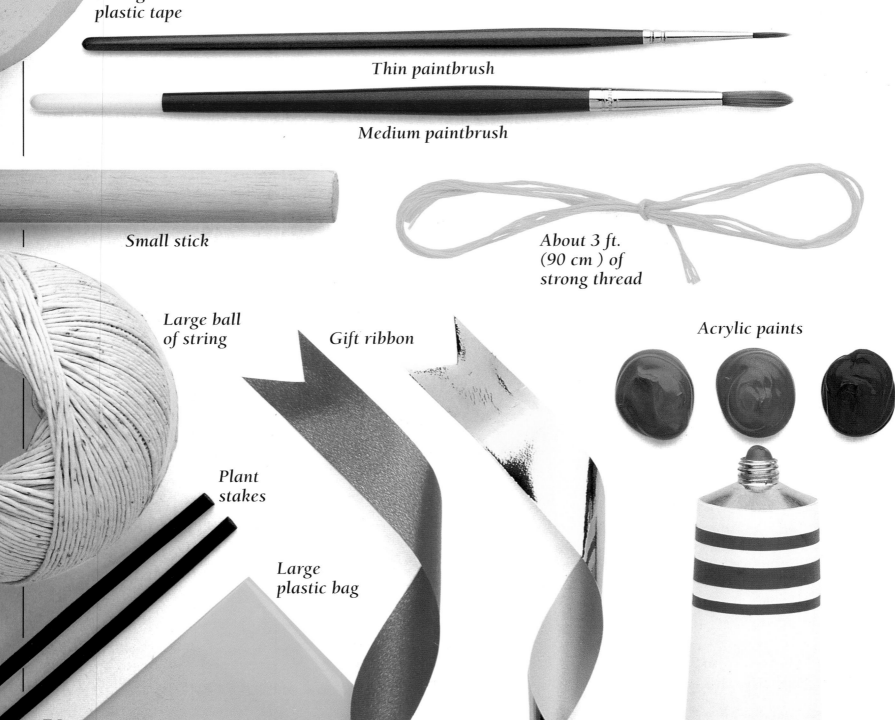

Strong plastic tape

Thin paintbrush

Medium paintbrush

Small stick

About 3 ft. (90 cm) of strong thread

Large ball of string

Gift ribbon

Acrylic paints

Plant stakes

Large plastic bag

Making the kite

1 Cut out a 19 in. (48 cm) square from a bag. Make three marks 5 ½ in. (14 cm) from the top, and three along the center, as shown.*

2 Join the marks on the edge of the plastic. Check that the plastic is ½ in. (1 cm) bigger than the stakes all around. Cut out the kite.

3 Stick tape (front and back) on the kite's corners and on the center line, 4 in. (11 cm) from the top and 3 in. (7 cm) from the bottom.

4 Fold each corner and punch through the folds to make two holes in each corner. Ask an adult to cut two slits on the center line.**

5 Paint a design on the kite and leave it to dry. Cut long pieces of gift ribbon. Hold them together and punch a hole in one end.

6 Turn the kite over. Thread one stake through the holes across the kite, as shown. Wrap tape over each end to hold the spar in place.

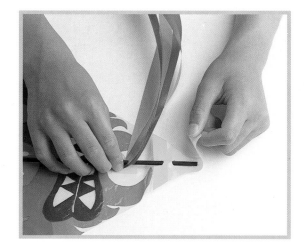

7 Thread the ribbons onto the other stake. Push it into the top and bottom holes, and under the first stake. Tape over the spar ends.

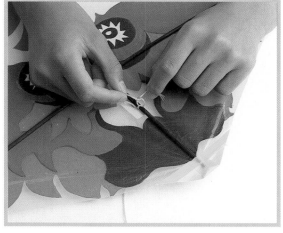

8 Turn the kite over. Push the ends of the thread through the slits in the kite's center and tie them to the upright spar at the back.

9 Tie a small loop in the thread. It should be at a right angle to the kite, as shown. This is the kite's bridle.

*Fold the plastic in half to find the center.
**Cut the slits through the tape pieces you placed in step 3.

FLYING DRAGON

Attaching the string

1 Wrap tape around each end of a small stick. Tie one end of a ball of string to the stick and wind on about 100 ft. (30m) of string.

2 When you are ready to fly your kite, tie the end of the string to the loop in the bridle. Knot it two or three times.

LAUNCHING THE KITE

When you want to fly your kite, make sure the string is tied securely to the bridle and stick. Find an open space. Unwind a little string. On a windy day, the kite should fly from your outstretched arm, or you can ask a friend to hold the kite at a distance and let go when it fills with wind. Once your kite is up, slowly let out more string.

Pull on the string and watch your kite rise up into the air!

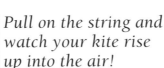

Stand with your back to the wind and hold the stick at each end.

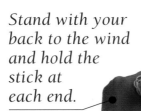

If your kite doesn't fly very well, try adjusting the angle of the loop in the bridle.

A long tail looks spectacular and keeps your kite steady. Red and gold ribbons suggest fire coming from the dragon's mouth.

The finished kite

You can copy this face or paint a different face on your kite – try an octopus, a lion, or a monster.

DOS AND DON'TS

• Never fly your kite in strong winds or stormy weather.
• Never fly near overhead cables, roads, cars, buildings, trees, people, animals, or an airport.
• Always wear gloves when kite-flying.
• Never look directly at the Sun and always wear sunglasses to protect your eyes.

The thick tape strengthens the plastic.

*The ends of the thread
are pushed through
the slits and tied to
the upright spar.*

*Make sure that the plant
stakes lie on the side of the kite
that isn't painted and that they
hold the plastic fairly taut.*

MAKING A COLLAGE

Everyday things can be used in a collage. Make a collection of materials that you think would look interesting. You don't have to use the materials shown: dried pasta shells, grains of uncooked rice, sand, fabric, string, and magazine cutouts are just a few more ideas.

Below, a city scene is made with collage materials. Turn the page to see the finished picture and for some ideas for different collages.

EQUIPMENT

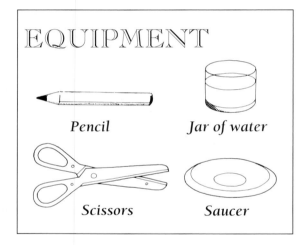

Pencil

Jar of water

Scissors

Saucer

You will need

Small box

White glue

Poster paints

Making the collage

1 Cut out and arrange your collage materials on cardboard to make a picture. Design the main parts of your collage first.

2 When you are happy with your picture, glue the materials on cardboard. Build up layers to make the collage stand out.

3 Different shapes and textures will add variety to your collage. Here, strips of corrugated cardboard form a pattern.

Thick cardboard

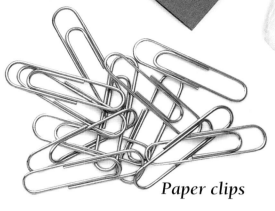

Thick and thin corrugated cardboard

Dried lentils

Paper clips

Cardboard egg carton

Paper drinking straws

Plastic drinking straws

Plastic plant tray

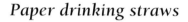

Dried spaghetti

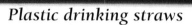

Thin paintbrush

Medium paintbrush

Painting the collage

1 When the g̶l̶... ̶r̶y, paint the collage. M̶... color with some white ... ̶e̶lp the paint coat the p̶... ̶r̶ials.*

2 Paint the background. You can build up texture by adding more white glue to the paint to thicken it.

3 Small things, such as paper clips or lentils, can be used to add detail. Stick them into the paint on the collage before it dries.

Mixing ⟍ glue also allows you to stick small things straight into the wet paint.

CITY SKYLINE

Here is the finished city scene. Tall buildings have been made with different types of cardboard and parts of a plastic plant tray. You can make a collage of anything you like: try a countryside scene, a picture of a farm, or the street where you live.

BACKGROUND

Stick your materials onto cardboard. Paper won't be strong enough to hold them.

STICKY PAINT

You can stick small things into the wet paint if it has been mixed with white glue.

Paper clips

Smaller buildings are stuck onto the taller buildings. This makes the taller buildings look as if they are in the distance.

Plastic plant tray

Plastic straws and strips of corrugated cardboard make a door.

Paper clips, pasta, or dried seeds can be arranged into interesting patterns.

Paint has been thickened with white glue to add texture to the cloudy sky.

Lentils

Dried spaghetti

Plastic
plant tray

You can leave some parts
of the collage unpainted.

CHOOSING COLORS

Think about the colors that you are going to use. Browns, grays, blues, oranges, and yellows have been mixed and used to paint the stone, brick, concrete, and metallic buildings in this city scene.

Part of a cardboard egg carton makes a perfect roof for this building.

Paper straws are used to make windows.

A FITTING FRAME!

The collage has been framed with corrugated cardboard. You can learn how to make this frame on page 47.

Thin strips of
corrugated card

Cardboard box

PAPIER-MÂCHÉ PINS

With some cardboard, papier-mâché, and poster paint, you can design and paint a pin in any shape you like: try making your favorite animal, machine, vehicle, a round face, a sun, or a moon. The finished pins make wonderful gifts for your friends or family.

To make the papier-mâché mixture for the pins, you need to tear newspaper into tiny pieces and then mix the pieces with a little water and wallpaper paste. It should be a very smooth, doughlike mixture. Leave your papier-mâché shapes to dry overnight before you start to paint them.

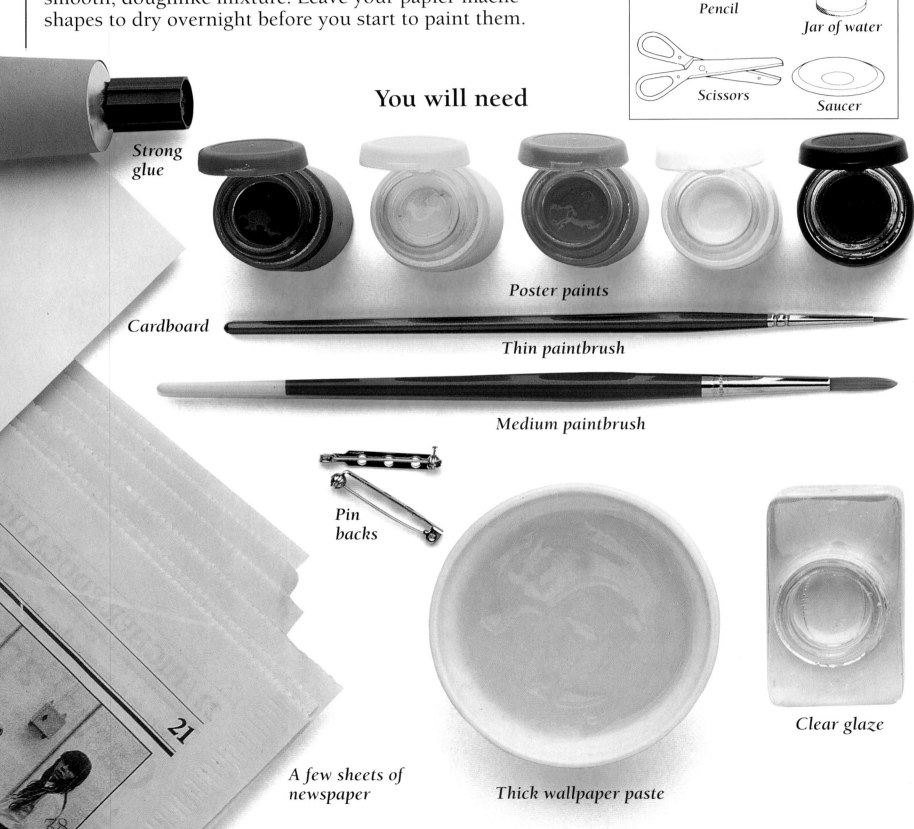

EQUIPMENT

Dish

Spoon

Pencil

Jar of water

Scissors

Saucer

You will need

Strong glue

Cardboard

Poster paints

Thin paintbrush

Medium paintbrush

Pin backs

A few sheets of newspaper

Thick wallpaper paste

Clear glaze

Making the pins

1 Draw a shape on cardboard and cut it out. Tear newspaper into tiny pieces and mix with water and wallpaper paste in an old dish.

2 Mash the papier-mâché until it has the texture of dough. Put some on the card. Shape the papier-mâché and leave it to dry overnight.

3 Paint a design on the front and paint the back one color. Leave the shape to dry. Glue on the pin back. Glaze the pin.

The finished pins

A thin paintbrush will help you paint detail on the small pins. Here are some different designs.

The glaze makes the pins stronger and gives a shiny finish.

BOAT

DINOSAUR

Here, papier-mâché has been shaped to look like fur.

DOG

SUN FACE

Papier-mâché was built up to make the frame on this pin.

FRAMED PICTURE

Leave one color to dry before you paint the next.

BUTTERFLY

CAR

MARBLING PAPER

Try making beautiful marbled papers and then use them to cover a folder. Marbling paper is great fun. Special paints are dripped into water and form patterns on the surface. You then place paper on the water to pick up the paint. Marbling paints are usually sold as part of a kit. You may need to thicken the water with a special powder before you drip in the paint, so check the kit's instructions. You can also use oil paints. Ask an adult to thin the paints with mineral spirits and add a little vinegar to the water.

EQUIPMENT

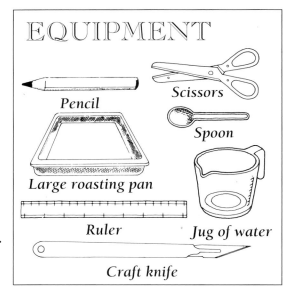

Pencil

Scissors

Spoon

Large roasting pan

Ruler

Jug of water

Craft knife

You will need

Ribbon

Two sheets of cardboard: ¹/₂ in. (1 cm) smaller all around than the marbled paper

White glue

Plastic drinking straws

Thickening powder*

Thick paper for inside of folder and flaps

Sheets of paper for marbling (These must be smaller than the roasting pan.)

Strong, wide tape

Marbling paints

40

*You may not need this: check the instructions with your kit.

Marbling the paper

1 Fill an old roasting pan with about 1 in. (2 cm) of water.** Use straws to drip a few drops of each paint color into the water.

2 Gently swirl the paint around with a straw to make a pattern in the water. Burst any bubbles on the surface with the straw.

3 Lay a sheet of paper on the surface of the water, holding it by opposite ends. Gently press down on the paper, as shown.

Making the folder

4 Lift up the paper and put it faceup on some newspaper to dry. If you used thickening powder, rinse the wet paper under water.

1 You will need two sheets of marbled paper to make a folder. Glue each sheet to cardboard to make the two sides of the folder.

2 Ask an adult to cut a small slit in both sides of the folder. Push a length of ribbon through each slit and glue down, as shown.

3 Tape the two outer corners on both sides of the folder. Then glue a sheet of thick paper to the inside of both sides of the folder.

4 Line up the sides of the folder, leaving a small gap between them. Join them together with two strips of tape. Make three flaps.***

5 Glue the flaps inside the folder on the right-hand side. There should be a tiny space between the flaps so that they fold over easily.

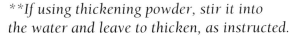

**If using thickening powder, stir it into the water and leave to thicken, as instructed.

*** Cut out and fold two flaps for the short edges of the folder and one for the long edge.

41

Marbled Folders

Choose tape and ribbon for your folder in colors that will go with your marbled papers. You can make different patterns every time you marble a sheet of paper. Experiment by swirling the paint in different directions, or leave it unswirled.

   You can also cover notebooks or diaries with your papers, use them as wrapping paper or to make gift bags and gift tags, or simply frame them as pictures.

Strong, wide tape around corners

Ribbon

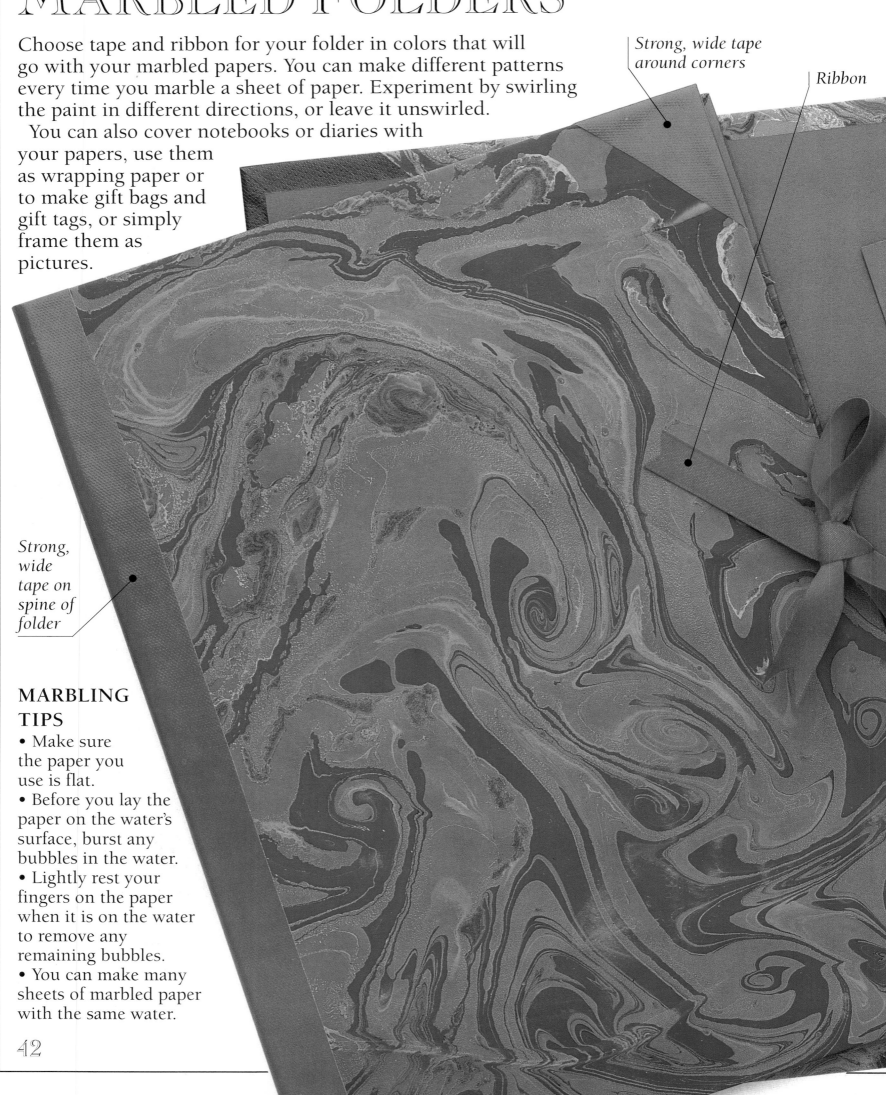

Strong, wide tape on spine of folder

MARBLING TIPS

• Make sure the paper you use is flat.

• Before you lay the paper on the water's surface, burst any bubbles in the water.

• Lightly rest your fingers on the paper when it is on the water to remove any remaining bubbles.

• You can make many sheets of marbled paper with the same water.

The two strips of tape joining the two sides of the folder together make a flexible spine.

The three flaps hold your paper or pictures in the folder.

Stick the flaps a little way in from the edge of the folder.

Thick paper is used to make the flaps.

43

SCRATCH AND SCRAPE

Try scraping marks into thick paint to make a textured painting. You can scratch out all sorts of different patterns. Use flour to thicken ready-mixed, water-based paints. Make sure that the flour is thoroughly mixed into the paint. When painting the picture, work quickly, or the paint will dry before you can scrape it!

EQUIPMENT

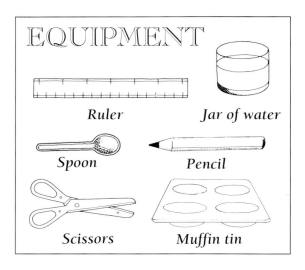

Ruler   Jar of water

Spoon   Pencil

Scissors   Muffin tin

You will need

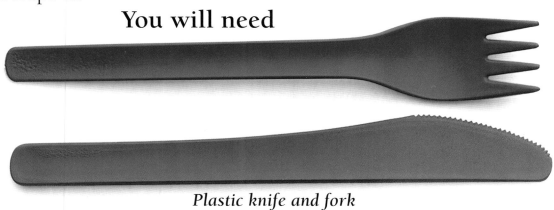

Plastic knife and fork

Paintbrush

Cardboard

Ready-mixed, water-based paints

Flour

White glue

44

Making the picture

1 Use a sheet of cardboard for the background. Draw shapes on another sheet.* Mix some flour into each paint color.

2 Paint the background. Quickly scrape different patterns into the paint with a plastic knife and fork. Do the same with the shapes.

3 When the background and shapes are dry, cut out the shapes, arrange them into a design, and glue them to the background.

Figure out what shapes you will need for your pattern on scrap paper first.

The finished picture

Here, diamonds and strips of cardboard have been arranged to make a colorful pattern.

Diamonds

Strips of cardboard

You can fit your shapes together like a jigsaw.

You can scrape swirls, straight lines, and different shapes into the paint.

This pattern was scraped with the teeth of a fork.

PAPIER-MÂCHÉ FRAME

Turn the page to find out how to mount and frame the picture.

White mount

45

FUN FRAMES

Frame your favorite paintings and hang them up at home. Below, you can find out how to make picture frames and how to make a "mount." This is the cardboard that surrounds a picture. You don't have to use a mount, but it can help a picture stand out.

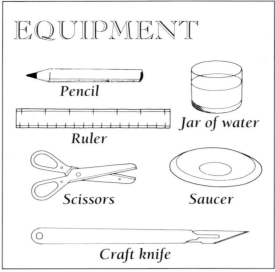

EQUIPMENT

Pencil

Ruler

Jar of water

Scissors

Saucer

Craft knife

You will need

Corrugated cardboard

Thick cardboard

Paintbrush

Poster paints

Strong thread

Papier-mâché

White glue

Plastic tape

46

Double frame

1 Draw a rectangle on cardboard ½ in. (1 cm) bigger all around than the picture you are framing.* Ask an adult to cut it out.

2 Ask an adult to cut out a narrower frame to fit over the first frame, as shown. Glue the frames together. Leave them to dry.

3 Paint the frame. Try printing, splattering, or scratching the paint. Tape the frame to some cardboard so that it dries flat.

*If your picture is square or round, draw a square or circle on the cardboard instead.

Mounting the picture

4 Glue your picture to a sheet of cardboard that is the same size as the frame. Glue the frame to the cardboard. Tape thread to the back.

Papier-mâché frame

Ask an adult to cut out a single cardboard frame. Then thicken the frame with papier-mâché.** Let it dry overnight and then paint it.

Corrugated frame

Cut out strips of corrugated cardboard. Glue them to a single cardboard frame, as shown. When the glue is dry, paint the frame.

**Turn to page 39 for instructions on making papier-mâché.

The frames

Paint your frame and choose a mounting cardboard in a color to suit the picture you are framing. Look at the frames on this page and on pages 13, 36, 45, and 48 for ideas.

CORRUGATED FRAME

PAPIER-MÂCHÉ FRAME

DOUBLE FRAME
Turn the page to see a printed double frame.

Scratched paint (see page 44 for this technique)

Splatter picture (see page 21 for splattering)

The white mount brings out the white in the splatter pattern.

FRAMING TIPS
• Make sure your picture is in the center of the frame.
• You can make the frame wide or narrow. Choose a width to suit your picture.
• If you are not using a mount, the frame hole must be slightly smaller than your picture.

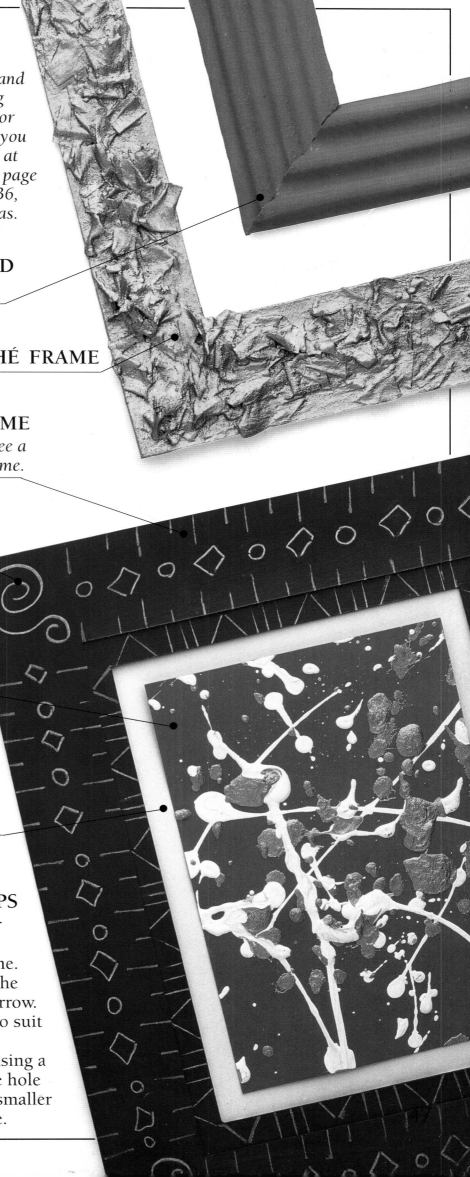

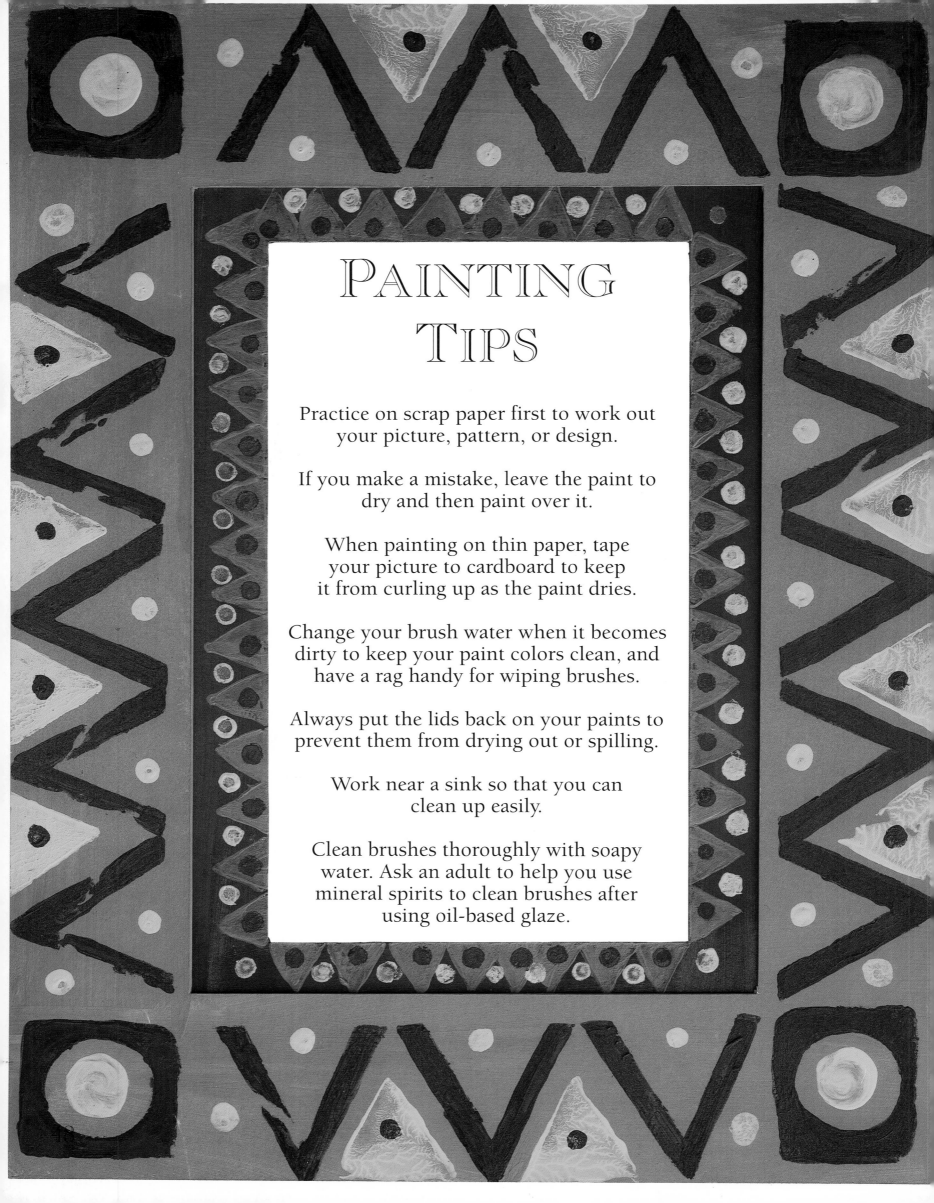

PAINTING TIPS

Practice on scrap paper first to work out your picture, pattern, or design.

If you make a mistake, leave the paint to dry and then paint over it.

When painting on thin paper, tape your picture to cardboard to keep it from curling up as the paint dries.

Change your brush water when it becomes dirty to keep your paint colors clean, and have a rag handy for wiping brushes.

Always put the lids back on your paints to prevent them from drying out or spilling.

Work near a sink so that you can clean up easily.

Clean brushes thoroughly with soapy water. Ask an adult to help you use mineral spirits to clean brushes after using oil-based glaze.